PUBLIC LIBRARY
STONEHAM, MASS.

for always

DRY SONGS AND SCRIBBLES
DONOVAN "Leitch"

Doubleday & Company, Inc., Garden City, New York
1971

821
L53d

credits:
photography:
    louisa johnson
    donald leitch
    donovan leitch
    david mills
illustration:
    donovan
design & art direction:
    sid maurer

The poems reproduced herein with
permission were written by Donovan Leitch
and were copyrighted by Donovan Leitch
and/or Donovan (Music) Ltd. during the years
from 1966-1969 inclusive except as to those
poems that are being published for the first
time in this book and are included in the
copyright thereof.

Library of Congress Catalog Card No. 70-147359
Copyright © 1971 by Donovan Leitch
All Rights Reserved
Printed in the United States of America
First Edition

AUG 18 1971

contents

POEMS 1964-1965
1965-1970

PROSE

1964-1965

Helen	yellow
Joan	vermilion
Joyce	grey
Vanessa	pink
Ann	gold
Tristy	silver
Ruth	white

poem   as   I   skirt   the   windy   street

cool   town
this   town
walk   down
              purple   starling   streets
              above
              a   soaking   sky
              a   weird   coldness   like
              steel   to   feel
         tangerine   harlequins   splashing
         from   a   pastel   play   moon
         twinkling   skin   of
              that   girl
                    browngirl
cool   town
this   town
walk   down
              the   sad   round   of   place
              names
         "we   could   paint   black-stick
         trees   on   the   grey   backcloth

         winter   evening

My love is a Mergirl
and spent on our love-bed of no-guilt love
I rise
with spangles in my eyes.
Her hair
at its longest
is soaked with my saliva.
her eyes twinkle
at my walking around the room
and I come near her once in a while
and touch her bare dusty feet
twisting her big warm body
against my love-play.
My eyes stroking her naked heart to nothing.
Grabbing her clothes
I throw them about the room
so I may see her
as she glides and stoops.

Beautiful sad evening river
hushing to the sea
Stoned out on beaches
stoned on you my Mergirl
so tangerine in her dusky park-walks with me
to quiet empty bandstand
with brass shrill in our minds
as we stand
deep in the leaves of sharp winter
warmly clothed with fishermen's jerseys
and cigarettes
in the jackdaw-grey winter evening
as we stumble in deserted children's swingpark
and the cold dull slide
and paint-flaking see-saw

Far in the stark landscape
to red-coated children
that tumble about the harlequin birch trees
the fine darkling sky
and sad wisps of words
her love-hand
in my love-hand
without touching

to work one day

dirty sheeps wool
hung on the skys' barbed wire
an' i stole a second
to feel the wind
pluckin' the pearl of the cold sun
in my fingers
i placed it behind my closed eyes
an' fell down the frosty steps
stainin' my hands red (faintly)
i joined the other tinned people
in the bus
to the factories
or soul destroyers
an' escaped
before i reached eight o'clock

did i hear a flutter of wings
or was it
rain in a drain
"you found somethin' here
didn't you?"
and i answered
"yes i did"
the confusion of autumn
colour in the woody leaves
crackling — spat under my feet

the most beautiful autumn
i've ever seen lay by
Meadow Studios

poem of a breeze

the moon
strolled across the
mauve an' purple air
of the damp evenin'
butterflys are dead
emotion of memory lies still
collar turned up
from cavern of yellow light
to cavern of yellow light
in the fog
a car crackles an' burns
its way by-thickly

thats not a miracle only a
green neon supermarket

summer
never lived
bewildered
I can hope for
a dead leaf that will
be as crimson-black
as the caught leaves
that I've seen —
blistered morgue photograph
of a
dead child
life and grass
in a tight new hand
all of you
bitterly confused

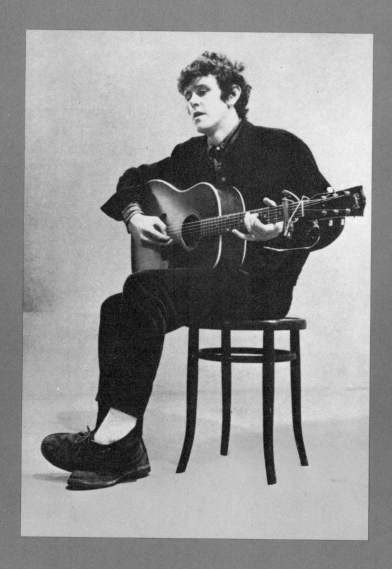

A new sound
in a new room
the "pip" of the
last raindrops as
I await the silence
of others asleep
and only then I creep
with roll-neck sweater
and clean — blue jeans
upon the cold of
night

to see where the
last hours rain has gone

red
bled the sea
with sunset

orange
slid out
on its pastel skin

blue
through the eye
was cool-
cloud
hustled
built up huge

a twist of tangerine harlequin
zapped across the night

christine is dead

the terror minutes
the poor child had
in the savage black eyes
smashed sex mind
of the cruel killer
the six summers of
her soft memory sparin'
her constructive thoughts
of twistin' fear
brain devoid of "why"
in the black stick
night of his mumbled speech
as he hurt her throat
with a knife
touched her downy flesh
fate spared her by death
for her life would
have been
a tangled reason

"The Firefly Dawn"

In the firefly dawn of friendly day,
In Autumn parks the children play,
Black crows tumble in the icy sky,
Hustlin', the dead trees sing an' cry.

In the firefly dawn of the angry door,
The pig in the sky is the moon's yellow whore,
In the nighttime last tide in mournin' black,
Sheets on the washin' line flap an' crack.

Red hand winds swoop an' curl,
The sun, in white, a sad grey pearl,
Froze in a pool of tepid 'ore,
The sound of eyes all spent an' sore.

In fierce splash rain, harsh an' hard,
Oppressed grass blades bent an' marred,
What is pain but no-mans ground,
An' memory is where tears run down

whisper in my pillow
that I never heard
have you ever felt
a tear wet hand
that tries to hold
your callous hand
because
you have to leave her —
broken speech hurled
at you
try to think of sunsets
an' it rains harsh tears
"Oh god I've run my make-up
you bastard"
people pass — the fog
swirls
I don't love you
I can't love you
break your nails in
my coat
"go back to your beatniks,
you phony"
I can't cry but cry dry

Ballad Called Two

I think
before we all die
we'll meet
together
in a dark pitch
child's swing park
we'll be apart
then we'll come
to the centre
of this silent swing park
and hold hands
Sam's hands that were
cold would be warm
dew glistenin'
in our hair
an' on our eyelashes
and
i think we will
cry together
very hard
an' our handgrips
will tighten
till
we hear the swings
creak with small
fingers an'
the roundabout
scrapes the gravel
till

voices sweet an' high pitched
shout an' mimic
across —
the darkness will retreat
an' go
till everythin'
a child — a young girl
with large eyes
will go with a
young boy
with black hair
to her home
an tell her mother
that two old women
an' two old men
held hands at the dawn
then parted
with memories
trailin' behind them
tryin' to connect
with the others'
trailin' memories
but
lyin' beaten
in a child's swing park
"an' mother,"
she'll say,
"i think they had no
faces to tell me what
they felt, mother
they had no faces"

bright paint
of mouth blood on the apple
in my hand
's on my hand
in vermilion
same as the young
teacher of children
who
drunk on stupid whiskey
splashed red
across my eyes
in her art room
I guarded her
from sweaty fingers who blouse-grope
guarded her
I took her though
in the dew sleep
of dawn
the note I left read
: teacher of children
I can't be with you always
take care — for the red
you splash isn't paint

around what

around
what was
churchill doin'
at the back
of a back
in the siege
of sidney street
the long coated guardsmen
shootin' at some
windows
in the flicker film
black
white
in the cellulose
memory of men

Ballad Called Three

twin flashes
of light
like the sun stared at
from behind a finger —
like the sun stared at
from behind lowered
eyelashes
a day of colour-less shadows
flashes of light
gossamer in their prismatic
construction
        twin flashes of
    light
and me
the bed of a river
polished and matt pebbles
the touch of the swallows'
beak on the surface of the
still pool

and grass
a cigarette butt
pushed into the soft mud
and the chatterin' wild
birds
the hazed figure
heavin' itself across
the far field
in the heat of the sun
the grass shoot
drainin' its tasteless cud
in my mouth
        twin flashes of
light — like the
sun seen through tear
filled eyes
tiny gossamer stars of light
  like the sun
   stared at from
     behind *her* finger
     like the sun

"Teracotta"

my cap
flung from my
head an'
drank from a puddle
in the January winds

St. James' park
flashed into focus
an' we huddled on a bench
our hands cut the air around
our three heads

all kinds of gulls
crowded the bread fingers
of rain coated people
feeding feeding feeding
we laughed in the breezes

armada of pink pelicans
left a wake of not so cool ducks
(rolled two under shelter)

beautiful crazy St. James' park
some man giggling at his
child's imagery
as the hashish
cleared our eyes

the riddle of birds
lay solved on the lake
beverly sat muted as always
by some kind of wordless speech
(bat who was fat once spat at a cat)

The winds howled cold
an' we dug the sensation
an' understood
you have to learn to be high and perceive

I ate more food this weekend
than I have ever eaten before

trigonometry sandwiches
on the buzz
in nearby Adalo
cuttin' clean
in the new June sunshine
the young girls
sweatin' nicely
on the hot feet
coca-cola signs
dry an metal
on old boards
(i stuck my wet hand
around my glass
like
they do)

Mumbling by
the tumbling tide
the king of America
humbly cried

Save ma soul
Save it soon
the king of America
fell in swoon

Little Linda

Little Linda glowing cinder
sparkle like a star
the sun and roses
merely show us
'zactly where we are
A jaguar a hollow car
far in the winter lane
lacework trees
the jack-frost breeze
pheasant birds are slain

I love the girl in white
and the Sun flashed gold in the rose sky

Come
I will show you beauty
enough to swell your heart

Come
cross the seas
the red-faced man in Soho
won't miss us
I don't dig going for bad trips about
each others feelings

If I run-follow me
Time is on our side
a mile wide
no place to hide
there's the cloud to ride
in Greece

Damp uncomfortable
Portabella market day
cold cutting winds
ruffled the velvet covered stalls
everybody is hustlin'

I buy a bloodstone ring
and smile in grey light
with a chilled lip thats taken a sip
of happiness

feel kissed
for i think of you

I feel a hunger and spin 'round
to see what it is and I can't
see anything
maybe you can help me

Draw a D in the dust on your shoe
in the little mainland dock in Greece
the sea distorted through bad glass
a little sweat in your palm
dry your hand on my hair
if I shut my eyes I can
wrap you in turquoise silk

I jumped
from concrete
and crunched on the pebble beach
a ghost beach
ragged sea-gulls
stinking dried sea-weed
clung like horror as
the sea gargled in
the damp mists
the slimy sewage break-
water lost itself far out

I'll go there
the road I left behind
disappeared
as the cockle boats shouted their muffled cries

a dream of little

on the beach
i rose before you
an' took the dog
to the shore
for driftwood
the cabin was hung
with a sleepy silence
your face in shadows
the heavy curtain
blocked the fine grey light
falling from the undecided sky

it's fresh outside
the dog is still drowsy
we gather driftwood
an' i feel good about you
i return an' creep in
the grey silence will break when
i light the fire
but before that
i kiss your eyes
my sea-beach breath
awakens you
very slowly
an' surely an' unafraid
for we both know now
an' this is the way we have
an' will come to pass

please make it come to pass
                    "Tristy"

seagull
green eyes
bill colour vermilion
filling cups with the
sound of eyes
poisoned wind evade
        and trade
with a nearby factory wall

sailed the boat into a pool
of silver by the sand
caves
a breeze blew in from the
nowhere
tremblin the waves
lappin to the sun
up the silver backstairs of the sky

the quiet afternoon

here are your eyes
i have them above me
in your photograph
strange that the drawer wouldn't open
(fade, fade, my how you'll fade)
why don't you talk
you're holdin' off

and if i look i can see
a brittle landscape (of the dead year)
i choose to remain empty

a puppet on the bleak and awful sand

shooting stars are seen
when stumbling from laughing cars
the faint tang of whyskey
in the menthol air
the stars hard
as diamonds lie on deep
velvet
the birds are all dead
a few will struggle with
the dawn
and start the new day

but that's tomorrow and
it may even snow again

I write to you this letter
at a late hour — a red hand
wind swoops the air out —
side — it even penetrated
the thick leather of my boots.
This letter must seem
strange — to hear from me
after I'd taken my path
and was gone.
(The strength of this letter
is not taken from the night
we spent sleeping) — I
apologize for keeping you
awake at the end of what
must have been a "large" evening
Gabby is a good crazy name
I await the blinding sight
of snow — it'll come.
There are some beautiful
quilts of dead autumn in
the woods here where I live
— a park with a sad red

bandstand — the trees have
lost their dusty barks to the
steel of winter — the pastel
sun affording no heat
pasted in grey sky
winter's strange dream of
metal sleep
Today I saw mosaic starlings
cut the air like hurled
daggers of iridescent feathers
(they looked scared)
Black Crows tumbled above
stark dead trees

my navel itches
how's your navel
that night I gazed
upon your navel
placed my finger in it

I like you

The Skipper

Oh in vain I wandered
and travelled the highways
Been bitten by Cold
as I slept on the breeze
starved in alleys where drunks
spill their stomachs
The night wind doth howl as I lie 'neath the trees

Dawn brings me round
and I walk without thinking
To streets of stolen milk
and broken old men
To the blocked eyes of young girls
all clean on the pavement
I shuffle in doorways till I don't know when

The day warms my blood
and evening is 'pon me
I burn all my time
in the great crowded nights
Till I'm alone and walking the dark streets
wishing for a home not the derelict sights

Never Settle Down

If I ever married an' settled down,
an' do no mo' ramblin' around,
you'd take my children off to war,
you wouldn't worry nothin' about
                    what they saw,
So I'll never marry an' settle down.

If I let your clocks tick out my time,
an' make me forget what's on my mind,
you'd make me do such terrible things
like a pawn on a chessboard like
                    a puppet on strings
so your clocks will never tick out my time.

If I ever played in your little game,
an' if I took heed to what you're sayin'
you'd give good reason why I should hate,
I'd believe in you till it was too late,
So I'll never play in your little game.
I'll roam my life from day to day,
I choose to live my life this way,
I can stand as tall as any man,
for you an' your kind I don't give a damn
I'll never never settle down
I'll never never settle down
I'll never never settle down

I've seen the plastic arm death
bubblin' slowly in the darkest
corners of the dusty room
big fever sounds screamin'
from the mouth pointin' south
in the Tate gallery
(in winter where the snow was
lyin' fine on the grass an' the
Thames was a cold steel gray
mirror an' we wandered
cold — shoutin' from the bridges
to the slidin' river below)
People can change but their faces
an' expressions never do when
feverishly recalled —
Two-week — Two-month or even
Two-year-old emotion don't
go down —
it's forgotten an' you can't
explain it — I remember an
old Nergo in an old railway pub
once said "The good book say
forgive but don't forget."

Song for the Sparrow Child in My Mind

The sparrow broke his wing one day
so bad he could not fly,
They took no time in tellin' him
that maybe soon he'd die.

The sorrow that he felt was
way beyond compare,
He saw from his own smeared
eyes sparrows flyin' everywhere.

He crept into the night so
dark he scarce could see
"A sparrow with one wing my friend"?
But at least he's free.

a terracotta love poem

velvet killed
its colour blue
for reds an' browns
upon your
beautiful arms
an' i can see you
shimmerin'
like a precious stone
playin' in the lights
of your eyes
i can soak my mouth
upon the ends of the
lowering cage
of your hair

As I peer out of one eye
and watch slow clouds go by
the sun be soon in bed
on pillows fluffy red
the tiny tinkling sound
of the small boy paper round

I muse the cast
of past acquaintance

1965 - 1968

Your voice is like the sound
of someone far behind
maybe Historians could hear

The Voyage of the Moon

The moon is like a boat my love
of lemon peel afloat my love
and with a sail of gauze my love
she seems to slightly pause
upon her silent way my love
all on her starry way

I see her pearly decks my love
set with diamond specks my love
I see her pearly mast my love
far from her sea-shell past
and softly does she sway my love
all on her starry way

Of silk they have been spun my love
her ropes that limply run my love
down to her carved prow my love
down to her mermaid prow

She seems to linger long my love
as if spell'd by a song my love
but no, she tarries not my love
her journey unforgot

All in the Sea of Sky my love
the Moonships sail and fly my love
and many are their kind my love

though all need but one wind
to make their starry ways my love
to make their starry ways

And there will come a time my love
O may it be in mine my love
when men will proudly rise my love
and board to sail the skies
Moonships from all spheres my love
Moonships from all spheres

The men be bathed in light my love
the women clothed in white my love
all in that wondrous fleet my love
as each the other meets
will smile and softly sing my love
will smile and softly sing

And on some distant sand my love
the ships will gently land my love
fair folk will meet them there my love
with flowing golden hair
and great will be their joy my love
great will be their joy

The moon is like a boat my love
of lemon peel afloat my love
and with a sail of gauze my love
she seems to slightly pause . . .

Easter Monday

Birds are singing trees awake
in a wood the lonely rake
Sits him down on springy bough
and Easter Monday's silent now

Seven, tolls a distant bell
the church wood floor where sermons fell
A wood dove claps the poet's line
with flapping wings and cooing fine

The rake he sits and ponders why
the Rook he thinks he'll up and fly
Folk think when to leave and how
and Easter Monday's silent now

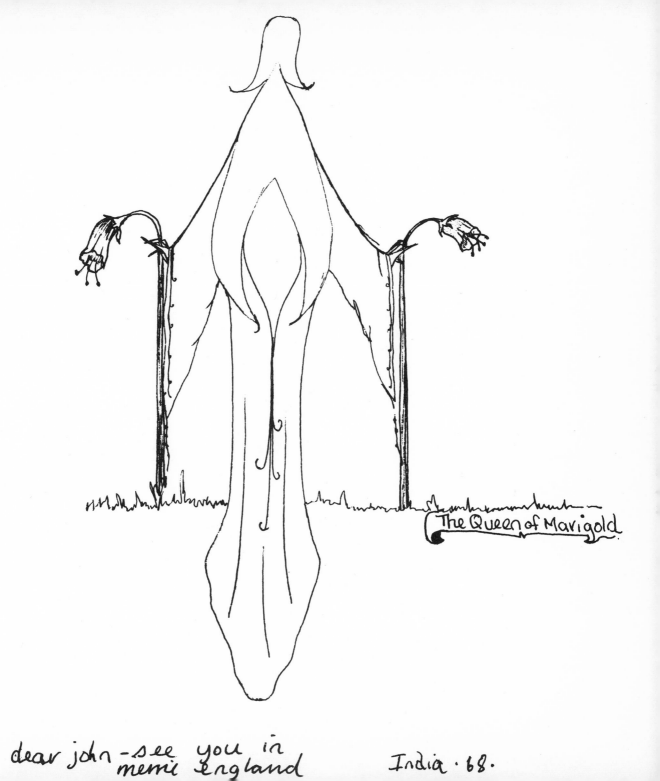

The Queen of Marigold.

dear john – see you in
memri England   India · 68.

I do not long for you
I long for me
a selfish man am I

Whether
we go on
together
or alone
one thing is for certain
it won't be for long

Today all the children
in the world must have
whispered
for a wind made me smile

India '68

Lord of the Reedy River

She fell in love with a swan
Her eyes were filled with feathers
He filled her with song
in the reedy river

She in her boat long hours
He in his royal plumage
She threw him some flowers
in the reedy river

Black was the night and starry
She loosened up her garments
and let fall her hair
in the reedy river

Sadly they mourn and sigh
whilst in evening twilight
two swans glide and fly
o'er the reedy river

India '68

Twas half a moon ago
I felt as though
my life would dim
should she go

Twas half a moon ago
I yearned to shew
all that is love
for I know

Twas half a dream ago
I learned to slow
although this truth
I well know

I awoke in the early hours
I opened my eyes
The net canopy over my bed
was of gold gauze.
I heard the sound of leaves
running in the night wind
like scatterred poems

India '68

Hold now, be not feart
Command imagined thought
Catch, if can, thy will
That swift so rarely caught

Forbid me not that which is mine
I am the heir 'Awaited Sign'
Scorn me not O witch of late
You heat the wax and seal your fate

I hurry not to build my boat
Upon the 'Sea of Thought' to float
Oak, and stout shall be my beams
I, master on the 'Deep of Dreams'

India '68

Will Our Visions of Tomorrow
Mingle With Those of Yesterday?

Verse 1

Come take a look with me
in an old fashion picture book
Patience, the girl we see
on the sand with her squint and her parasol, look
sweet herbs are sewn
'tween the cloth of her cuffs
a shell in her little tight hand
soon she'll be going away with her
Bottled sands Tomorrow from the Shores of Yesterday

Verse 2

Come see her move and be
in our old fashion backward look
Just like an old movie
talking and real like when it was took
bat balls and town boys cheeky and rough
faint sounds of a distant brass band
who rides the donkey today, will our
Visions of Tomorrow mingle with those of Yesterday

Verse 3

Come close your eyes and hear
melodies from an old music box
Tinkling as tendems and years
go tumbling like tresses and small perfumed locks
sweet dreams were sewn
'tween the years of her life
a tear in her little kerchief
waiving and fading away, with her
Bottled sands Tomorrow from the Shores of Yesterday
Oh will our visions of Tomorrow mingle with those of Yesterday?

Jack Daw

Jack Daw
saw
the sparkle

And sigh
did
he warkle

The sky
it
did darkle

Greed had
he
for sparkle

He saw
ring
in twignest

To serve
as

he
in treebest

Jill daw
proud
in twignest

Jack Daw
'pon
a strayday

Take care
did
the dove say

Search well
all
the skyway

Jack Daw
'pon
a strayday

Epistle to Derrol

Come all ye starry starfish
dwelling in the deep blue sea
Crawl to me I have a
proposition to make thee
Would you walk the North Sea floor
to Belgium from England
Bring me word of a Banjo Man
with a tattoo on his hand

The spokesman of the starfish
spoke as spokesmen should
If'n you met our fee
then certainly we would.
Should you cast a looking glass
upon the scalloped sand
you'll have word of this Banjo Man
with the tattoo on his hand

Come ye starry starfish
I know your ways are caped.
Maybe it's because you're
astrologically shaped.
Converse with the Herring shoals
as I know you can.
Bring me word of the Banjo Man
with the tattoo on his hand

The eldest of the starfish
spoke after a sigh
Youthful as you are young man
you have a Wisdom Eye.
Surely you must know
a looking glass is made from sand.
These young stars are fooling you
about your Banjo Man

Come then aged starfish
riddle me no more.
For news I am weary
and my heart is sore.
All on the silent seashore
help me if you can.
Tell to me if you know
of the Banjo Man

All through the seven oceans
I am a star most famed
Many leggys have I lost
and many have I gained
Strange to say, quite recently,
I've been to Flemish land
and if you are courteous
I'll tell you all I can

You have my full attention
I answered him with glee
His brother stars were twinkling
in the sky above the sea
So I sat there with rapt
attention on the sand
Very anxious for to hear
of the Banjo Man

I have seen this tattooed hand
through a ship's porthole
Steaming on the watery main
through the waves so cold
Heard his tinkling banjo
and his voice so grand
but you must come to Bel-gi-um
to shake the tattooed hand

Gladly would I come
O gladly would I go
had I not my work to do
and my face to show
and I rejoice to hear he's well
but I must go inland
thank you for the words you brought
of my Banjo Man

I walked along the evening sand
as charcoal clouds did shift
Revealing the moon shining
on the pebble drift
Contemplating every other word
the starfish said
Whistly winds they filled my dreams
in my dreaming bed

John

Must you lay down your fate
to the Lord High Alchemy
In the hands of the chalk and the Drug
Magic circles he will spin
and dirges he will sing
through the transparency of a
           Queen Ant's Wing

~ John ~

Writer in the Sun

The days of wine and roses
are distant days for me
I dream of the last and the next affair
and of girls I'll never see
and here I sit, the retired writer in the Sun

Tonight I trod in starlight
I excused myself with a grin
I ponder the moon in a silver spoon
and the little one alive within
and here I sit, the retired writer in the Sun

The magazine girl poses
on my glossy paper aeroplane
too many years I spent in the city
playing with Mr. Loss & Gain
and here I sit, the retired writer in the Sun

I bathe in the Sun of the morning
lemon circles swim in the tea
fishing for time with a wishing line
and throwing it back in the sea
and here I sit, the retired writer in the Sun

Isles of Greece

The Long Dawn

Daylight came
to my living brain
in the house of thought
the master

Loss and gain
were deftly playin'
the game of
dodge disaster

A troubled look
from the mirror shook
a finger at
a sky swift

A rook-thief took
the sometimes book
as I watched
the sand sift

Two Lovers

When two lovers touch hands
they touch the two of them
touching hands
they touch the one of them
in the space between
as each the other's hand doth touch

When two lovers kiss lips
they kiss the two of them
kissing lips
they kiss the one of them
in the space between
as each the other's lip doth kiss

When two lovers hold each other
they hold the two of them
holding each other
they hold the one of them
in the space between
as each the other holds

Little pebble upon the sand
now you're lying here in my hand
how many years have you been here
Little human upon the sand
from where I'm lying here in your hand
you to me are but a passing breeze
and the Sun will always shine where we stand
depending in which land we may find ourselves
now you have my blessing go your way

The Song of the Naturalist's Wife

Do I see you coming home
    coming home to me
Could it be you that I see
    coming home to me
From your day by the sea

Do I see your pockets full
    pockets full of shells
Could it be you that I see
    pockets full of shells
From your day by the sea

Do I see you weary weave
    weary weave your way
Could it be you that I see
    weary weave your way
From your day by the sea

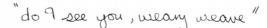

"do I see you, weary weave"

Isle of Islay

How high the gulls fly o'er Islay
How sad the farm lad deep in play
felt like a seed on your land

How well the sheep's bell music makes
Rovin' the cliff when fancy takes
felt like a grain on your sand

How blest the forest with bird song
How neat the cut peat laid so long
felt like a tide left me here

In a silent canadian wood
I walked
the cold air was still and fresh
Autumn's brilliant costumes
lay strewn
about the slender ankles of her
naked trees

The Ferris Wheel

Walking in the sea-shore twilight
It's then you spy Carnival lights
You slowly near the magic sight
Tangerine sky (minus one kite)

Take time and tie your pretty hair
The gypsy driver doesn't care
if you catch your hair
in the ferris wheel and turn

A silver bicycle you shall ride
To bathe your mind in the quiet tide
Far off as it seems your hair will mend
With a Samson's strength to begin again

Take time and dry your pretty eyes
Watch the sea-gull fly far off skies
to build its nest
in the ferris wheel and turn

Catch the Wind

In the chilly hours and minutes
of uncertainty
I want to be
in the warm hold of your loving mind

To feel you all around me
and to take your hand
along the sand
ah, but I may as well try and catch the wind

When sundown pales the sky
I want to hide awhile
behind your smile
and everywhere I'd look your eyes I'd find

For me to love you now would be
the sweetest thing
'twould make me sing
ah, but I may as well try and catch the wind

When rain has hung the leaves with tears
I want you near
to kill my fears
to help me to leave all my blues behind

Standing in your heart is where
I want to be
and long to be
ah, but I may as well try and catch the wind

Good Morning Mr. Wind

Where are you going
O wind of the morning
Your slippers are showing
And you're still yawning?

To waken the wee-ones
And tickle their lashes
For breakfast of milk-buns
Toy spoons and splashes

Where are you going
So tinily singing
And where are you blowing
The kiss you are making?

To ponds to make ripplings
To blow out the matches
And lift up the gull wings
When the plough scratches

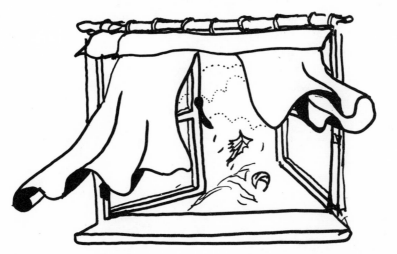

Sweetheart

It is night and a dog barks in his darkness in the farm
beyond the wood.
I smell the Sea in the wind and the small stream which
runs by the cottage, I hear.
I have your beautiful letter before me.
I would prefer to answer your words with kisses and
embraces because it is difficult to find words to say
what only holding can.

I shall come for you to come with me and be my love
when the leaves are falling to their golden death
and the snow clouds assemble in the white north
I shall kiss the spring into your wintry eyes and wrap
you in sheeps' hair and we shall watch the rooks
tumble in the bare trees.
Logs we shall burn and drink hot juices
and we shall sleep as snug as rabbits
as the wind rushes through trees chasing the moon
down the sky

O daffodil in yellow splendarrayed
who from the winter glass house often strayed
to blow your trumpet smell for penny worth
and cheat the season of your rightful birth

Full and proud your clustered choir doth stand
but do I see you bound by nurs'ry hand
useless there in faucet water still
and not in tree-foot sleep upon the hill

Tis I who bought your blaze to please my eye
tis them who caught your sprays and made you die
tis gold that is your colour and your worth
and men that cheat the season of your birth

The Lullaby of Spring

Rain has showered far her drip
splash and trickle running
Plant has flowered in the sand
Shell and Pebble sunning

So begins another spring
green leaves and of berries
Chiff-Chaff eggs are painted by
mother bird eating cherries

In a misty tangled sky
fast a wind is blowing
In a new born rabbit's heart
River Life is flowing

So begins another spring
green leaves and of berries
Chiff-Chaff eggs are painted by
Mother bird eating cherries

From the dark and whetted soil
petals are unfolding
From the stony village kirk
Easter bells of old ring

So begins another spring
green leaves and of berries
Chiff-Chaff eggs are painted by
mother bird eating cherries

wish I now were off some Island
casting nets to catch the fish
Clothéd in a tangled sheep coat
singing songs and catching fish

A night of moonbathers

the gardener said the storm last
night blew sand from Africa
and that's why the cars today were
all spotted

Also pink hailstones fell as big as
goose eggs in Cardiff
and they put a few in a fridge
to prove it

And he should know cos he swam
before and after lunch in "madam's"
pool

It was 90° in the shade today
and London was heavy with humid air
like Athens or L.A.
all the cars drove slowly — but I missed
the hurricane lamps in the little cafes

Everybody must have cut the lawn
today cos the smell of grass filled
the suburb streets

In the country though
I stand
drunk with the flowers breath
the night continues
hot

albatross and gannets

I remember very well
Longago from within a shell
I did hear the sea call
to Gannets in a free fall

the child tastes the sea
in the tear that you shed, and
the child feels the pain in the dream
that swims by
and he may or may not know
but he will when he finds his own
Lady of the Lemon tea

Sails on the Sea
wheels on the Land
cannot carry me further than I stray
from your hand
and the gift I must leave you is the
burden you carry my
Lady of the Lemon tea
out there on loneliness hill
with sadness and sorrow
your companions still
I'll be there at the end of your life
I'll be there
and we'll leave human sorrow behind

The Magpie

The magpie is a most illustrious bird
dwells in a diamond tree
One brings sorrow and one brings joy
sorrow and joy for me

The magpie is a most royal bird
black and blue as night
I would that I had feathers three
black and blue and white

I saw the gentle magpie birds
in dusky yester eve
One brought sorrow and one brought joy
and sooner than soon did leave

The magpie is a most illustrious bird
dwells in a diamond tree
One brings sorrow and one brings joy
sorrow and joy for me

don't look now
your vision is impaired by fatigue
your body is yearning
for love in the morning
you've journeyed now many a league

don't look now
your senses are blunted by what you see
your body is aching
at worst when you're waking
you recall that once you were free

don't look now
you're being followed by future events
your body is hoping
and faithfully coping
your nightmares galloping

your winter of changes relents
at times
with the promise of spring
from the wet mouth of spring
let joy gulls take wing
let reedy winds sing
let it be the same kiss saturate thee
for truth grows
        at the tip of
                your nose
and the truth of the morning
silent forlorning
your bed body longing
your heart weary song sing
the passage of time slips unseen
through overgrown gardens
              of dreams

Enid with Child

O Enid with child is round and good
and sleeping very deep
in shallow shores under sun
moving in her belly dream
(in the rain but no Gene Kelly seen)
Clumsily pretty with babies in her mouth

O Enid with child is soft and mine
and loving very real
if real be short for 'regarding all'
Groaning in her echo sleep
above me on the bed

O Enid with child is pickled and canned
in her salmon dream pink ice cream
(a living fertility goddess)
Knitting a cradle with her toes dipped in sleep

Enid with child

O Enid with child is too far gone
and happy are we that it's so
to recreate for God we feel proud
and this is all

O Enid with child is round and warm
dreaming that a kiss ate her up
all the stars race down the sky
floundering spices catch her eye
as she saves a jar of sauerkraut
from its boredom on a delicate shelf

O Enid with child is lying there
curled like a child beneath her hair
hurled like a star in her vast sleep
Like a doll in a doll
though she soars from her deep
to the 'Twelves' minor E, and returns

O Enid with child needs holding

O Youthful Mother

O Youthful Mother
shape upon your lap
dozing as the embers settle down
Rest you now
for you have but to be
Rest now from all thought
of things you sought

Youthful Mother
shape upon your lap
Creating all through the day
all through your sleep
making the one to make us three

May God bless our babe
and you
and me

Just to arrange the thoughts so strange

tough one — tight time — no rhyme
has been — won't much — longer be
change train — blues rain
brella — um pity boom zoom
plane board — stiff bored
let love
letter love — no love
Dear heart — yours, Don . . p . s . . . nothing
    a scene — what —
dream build — card house
all fall — jokers all
day grey cottage wave
rose tree murder
enter magic balloon carriage
be cool in cool

turquoise sky fill my eye
meditate feel feel feel
real real we all
in the quiet of pot bubbling stew night
    darkness falls — light falls down
the slope of the world

all the creatures prepare for the
black hours in holy worship

deep silent night
behold — the renegade wind.

Young Girl Blues

It's Saturday Night
it feels like a Sunday in some ways
If you had any sense
you'd maybe go 'way for a few days
Be that as it may
you can only say you are lonely
You are but a young girl
working your way through the phonies

Coffee on
milk gone
such a sad light and fading
Yourself you touch
but not too much
you've heard it's degrading

The flowers on your stockings
are wilting away in the midnight
The book you are reading
is one man's opinion of moonlight
Your skin is so white
you'd like maybe to go to bed soon
Just closing your eyes
if you're to rise up before noon

High heels
car wheels
the losers are grooving
Your dream
strange scene
images are moving

Your friends they are making
a pop-star or two (or three) every evening
You know that scene backwards
they can't see the patterns they're weaving
Those friends are all Models
but you soon got over that one
You sit in your one room
a little brought down in London

Caf'e on
milk gone
such a sad light and fading
Yourself you touch
but not too much
you've heard it's degrading

Widow with Shawl
(a portrait)

Dear wind that shakes the barley fre
Blow home my true love's ship to me
fill her sails
I aweary wait upon the shore

Forsake her not in times of storm
Protect her oaken beams from harm
fill her sails
I aweary wait upon the shore

Whether he be in Afrika
Or deep asleep in India
fill his dreams
I aweary wait upon the shore

Seven years and seven days
No man has seen my woman ways
dear God
I aweary wait upon the shore

And in my chariot of sleep
I ride the vast and dreamy deep
deep sea
I awake aweary on the shore

Dear snow-white gulls upon the wing
I, like you, am lamenting
for my love
I aweary cry upon the shore

Along the shingle beach I go
The wind about me as I make
my way
To my weary dream upon my bed

Legend of a Girl-Child Linda

I will bring you gold apples
and grapes made of rubies
that have shone in the eyes of
a Prince of the Breeze

Bright cascading crystals
they dance in the sand —
dunes on the beach of no footprints
to harpsichord tunes

A throne of white ivory
a gown of white lace
lies still in the magic
of a timeless place

One hundred small children
they laugh at the white doves
as they rest on their hands
with the touch of love

On a hillside of velvet
the children they lay down
and make fun of the grown-ups
with their silly frowns

And the sound of their laughter
is the sound of the green
sea as it washed round the foot of
the Sea-shell tree

The doves circle over
and land in the trees
where parrots are talking
their words with such ease

Thus spoke three Wizards
to the young ones that day
"There's sadness in the kingdom
make it go far away

If you follow the sunbeams
through the Valley of Flowers
to the Palace of the White Queen
with the white jade tower"

The youngest she sighed and
the clouds drew away;
one hundred small fingers
scratched their heads in dismay

From out of the Sun a
giant Gull came flying
and the children got ready
to sit on its wing

They waved to the raindrops
as they soared o'er the trees
The wind tossed their hair high
flashing gold on the sea

They came to a castle
and there they did fall
And they saw all the sadness
through the crystal wall

A princess lay sleeping
so gentle and kind
Whilst her prince took to battle
with his confused mind

The clash of bright metal
brought the children fear
but their cloaks of blue satin
dried up all his tears

The children held hands and
they spelt out her name
All the golden children
became a golden chain

It lies on a white throne
in a magic place
With a tunic of velvet
and a gown of white lace

My sword it lies broken
and cast in a lake
In a dream I was told that
my princess would wake

Little Ben

Rain on a window
Kettle on a stove
Where is little Ben
In the Rowan Grove

Tide on the turning
Davey on the sea
where is little Ben
he's with me

My name's Gwindle
in scarlet livery
I'm the Rowan Fairy
who dwells in this tree.

The Tinker and the Crab

On the windy beach
the sun is shining through
with weather fair.

White horses riding
on the sea pasture
onto the sand.

Over the dunes came a travelling man.
Sack on back wild flowers in his hand.

Old rusty cans
pebbles bedded in the sand
stand and stare.

Scratching his beard
through the grass he steered
his sandy shoe.

Disappearing in the dips
pondering and wan-
dering along.

Nice as you please comes the travelling man.
Drinking a bottle of milk in his hand.

Speaking to no-one
in particular
but happily.

Down where yon gulls
dance, driftwood lying, drying
for the fire.

Yellow beak and sleek
now the gulls are crying,
flying higher.

Out from the sea came a little green crab.
Taking the sun the morning being very drab.

Old rusty cans
pebbles bedded in the sand
stand and stare.

Christo

I was born of Winifred in the time of woe
And I go where I go and I know what I know

Yea, though I ride in some dark strange land
Wherever I go I feel my friend Christo

Go where I may he is always there
With his black curling hair and his sea-grey eyes so fair

For the love of women there has been a break
O such a lot of time those dear creatures do take

Now I am the father of a baby boy
May his days be filled with sun and his nights filled with joy

Younger days have gone we have become as men
Though we dearly hold on to a time way back when

Fishing harbour smells and full days of joy
Still, my son will play with your son one day

Teaching them to rock climb and to cry like gulls
And their days will be storms when our days will be lulls

One day I will settle and I'll raise my doves
As he shares in my life so he'll share in my loves

And when I've found out all I wish to know
There by my side will be my friend Christo

Off we will go with our blanket bed
Off in search of the end where our life paths have led

Here lies a minstrel by name Dono
And here by his side lies his dear friend Christo

The wild flowers
of the field — as the gulls rest
on the crags — gorse grows
the sky's rose — darkens
and the little old lady
(the red queen) in the INN
with the tea-cosy heart
chatters

hands tingling
cigarette smoking
                    Skye '68

Timothy timid came to town
With his face all hanging down

Flute in a pocket
hole in a shoe
Bead hanging on a neck
timid as a shrew

Wings of skin
Bay of peace
Lambs asleep
'neath tangled fleece

Dreams on the tumble
of feathers made
Rise up high and fall like lead

Ladies to Curtsey
Gentlemen bow
take your partners
for the changes now

Buy my cabbages
cheap and green
Buy my bacon
good and lean

Buy my shiny nails
long and strong
Swing that hammer boy
swing that song

I see you see
We'll all be free
Isay Mingay
and Clett makes three

On my right hand all is well
On my left hand all is well.

Skye '69

the wind does shake the
caravan and the little black
velvet dog curls down
in his little night
preparations.

Skye '69

Aug. 14, '69, Skye

morning   the loch is outside again
this morning
and Rosie is shocked to find
a small blister at the entrance
to her gates of joy
(I feel proud, as you can imagine
our very first blister)

evening   I don't think people want to
order their day into some soft
symmetry
to have a pause

but they reveal in their chaos

Aug. 17, '69, Skye

wild wet and windy Sunday
last night a wasp stung Rosie
on the breast
we are cosie
this day is a dreamy way
of pouring over maps of exotic
lands and far away seas

Aug. 18, '69, Skye

After stormy tempestuous
night
which broke quiet black star
night
a windy white crest waved
sea fresh cloud blue sky
lovely scottish day like
dreamt of and much loved

Aug. 19, '69, Skye

Woke in rose curtain room gloom
'always', I let out and cut an
ice cold orange from our Canadian
fridge
Rosie awoke with little bursts of
gurgling — she smoothed her fingers
between my legs
we made hot love
then dreamt of eggs — and
the Caribbean seas
black sands — chalky yogis
the winter when it comes
to the little lilac cottage

I must have her checked over
(she dismissed herself from hospital
after a broken nose and has
suffered from a cold for two years)

Silly girl — I love her

I am a poem
I live in a book
open the page
and take a look

Seeking Sorrow's Joy
there go you, go I
wandering are we
lovers yet to be

Seeking love to find
weary rivers wind
soon to become one
shining in the Sun

In the lands where there is no wind
That is the earth when she's breathing in
And in the lands where there is no drought
That is the earth when she's breathing out

Memory

we stood upon the bridge
so high above the river
suspended from the slopes
and looked at the toy tugs
far below

we tossed our pennies over
so far did they fall
floating and spinning down
out of sight and splash
far below

the bridge over the water
so high above the river
the cottage now in ruin
the ferryman has gone
far away

thurs-night 18 feb

the snow has all gone
and the night is moonlit
low clouds scud fast
across the blue sky
before a good clean wind

fri-night 19 feb

the wind has flown
heavy rain just falls
steadily

There is an Ocean

there is an ocean
of vast proportion
and she flows within ourselves

to take dips daily
we dive in gaily
he knows who goes within himself

the abode of angels
the mystical promised land
the one and only heaven
the god of man

is but the closing of an eye-lid away

there is a silence
of pure excellence
and she flows within ourselves

to appreciate
we de-activate
he knows who goes within himself

the domain of devils
the fearfull land
the only hades
the satan of man

is but the closing of an eye-lid away

all is as it was and ever more shall be
though they try to tell us it's not so
over all the earth there's nothing new to see
accepting every seed will newly grow
innocence of childhood base men misconstrue
to be years of darkness spent in shade
denying childhood's vision of the god of love
so that truth be turned about and untruth made

there is a reason
for every season
of change within ourselves

to navigate
we appreciate
and know the flow within ourselves

the deliverence from deluge
the good dry land
the only haven
the rock of man

is but the closing of an eye-lid away

The Garden of Truth

In the Garden of Truth there lived a bird
with feathers of a yellow gold
and all through the day the Sun did play
upon his raiment gay

In the Garden of Truth there lived a bird
with feathers of a silver pale
and all night long the Moon she shone
upon her raiment wan

And all within the branches of a great Oak tree

that some call the Tree of Life
and the Wise Men they come
to rest upon
the roots and to hear the songs

Moon
you are a reflection of the sun
poets in thy fashion shine upon
beautiful believers in the ore

sailing homeward
it's time to go home
over the oceans of life
we must roam
and when you get there
say hello for me
for i've a long, long way to go

there will be stormy days
there will be fine
there will be valleys
with mountains to climb
and when you get there
say hello for me
for i've a long, long way to go

whenever i wander weary
i'll reach for you
i know you'll be there
for to see me through

Hotel Juliet

In the Hotel Juliet
at a little table sat
Lady sipping Vichy
beneath a Lemon tree

In the Hotel Juliet
in the south of France they met
but that was long ago
the memory told her so

In the Hotel Juliet
salada vinegrette
receiting by the sea
Rimbaud poetry

In the Hotel Juliet
she dreamed with no regret
a friendly half carafe
an ancient phonograph

In the Hotel Juliet
at a little table sat
sentimental Lady
beneath a Lemon tree

DONOVAN 1969

Porthole

I see everything as it is
now that my windows are round
I see all the things that I missed
now that my windows are round

they keep out the water
they let in the Sun
the moon on the water
when the day is done

How silly the politician looks
wearing his public smile
trying to hide his incapacity
when it's sticking out a mile

with his paper-mãché wife
and their paper trashy life
if he sees himself as the man for the job
his mirror's telling lies

How silly the priest or parson looks
striking a holy pose.
trying to hide his nakedness
with medieval clothes

he's holdin' a golden key
but what it looks like to me
they're holding all the real-estate
thats your neighbourhood poverty

these are just a few of the things I've been noticing
dear politician priest or parson if you really feel like helping
open up your heart
that at least's a start
open up your heart
that's the helping part

How silly the queen of england looks
sipping her royalty
the essence of non-cimmittallness
in the grand democracy

it's the hanovarian strain
erin's isle is not the same
for the poets rhyme
she gives us wine
we hope for better things from charles

these are just a few of the things I've been noticing
your royal majesty dear madam if you really feel like helping
open up your heart
that's the helping part
let your xmas message start
"open up your hearts"

How silly the politician looks
wearing his public smile
How silly the priest or parson looks
striking a holy pose.
How silly the queen of england looks
sipping her royalty
How silly, How silly, How silly

The European Dream

I don't know where I go when i sleep
I wake up and I wonder where I've been
I look around and realise where I am
Forgetting where I'm resting it would seem

I woke up in a hotel room like in that Bergman film
The room was very strange and alien

A heavy hipped lithograph hung on Marie Antoinette grey
I did not know whether t'was night or day
Hello happy Anna
pigeon-english-toed
Jangling telephone ring
go on with the show
One-eyed grey hairs waiter
bring me Chivas Regal
Drown my sorrows deep
disney cheese and coffee
Victoriana bath chamber
nineteenth century
European Hotel
I'm in a Bergman Movie
Past the dusty curtain
quiet-eyed to the street
Overcoated people
walk by wint'ry trees
I may never leave here
captive in the past
I'm lonely dreaming
icicles don't last
Austrian Ice Champion
fresh-eyed rosy cheek
Secret message tapping
through the pipes she speaks

(the vision)
Surfacing from deep sleep
unknown wilderness
Clinging in the dream state
to a thread of conciousness
Surrealistic still life
French mock-antique decor
Frozen in my doom-bed
as the visions pace the floor
The bed was on a small stage
the curtain hung apart
Ghosts of strange assortment
at a private opera
The drama was then reversed
a phantom cast, they played
Advancing from the shadows
as Awareness did fade
Calling arms to action
I toiled to no avail
Movement none could I make
nor shun the phantom wail

To combat the creeping fear
Forcing Iris open
I willed my father near
Sleep at last o'er comes me
safety in defeat
Once again 'tis morning
car horns in the street
Overcoated people
face-less by wint'ry trees
Victoriana Bathchamber
nineteenth century
European Hotel
I'm in Bergman movie

The Crunch

Now we have come to the crunch fellow man
All that we own is all that we are
Factories and Cities depressing and grey
Guaranteed Free from all that's light and gay

Polluting the water we're required to drink
Polluting the air we're required to breathe
Stop! cries the protest group and the government sends police
They have shares in the Factories would you believe

Complete and utter disragard
for what is wild and free
He looks on in his ignorance
the common man he sees
blames the weather
toasts the cheese
on his knees

Take a look at the facts open up your eyes
We may hide the truth, we cannot hide the lies

Pollution means the plague, Middle Ages again
And all of the soaps and toothpaste won't clean us then
We're travelling through the space on this globe we call Earth
All in perfect harmony with the myriads of stars
All of this fighting about who gets to sit where
When it doesn't really matter it's the same ride there
And now we have come to the Church

Poorman's Sunshine

Outa the water and into the air
Outa the water and into the air
Outa the womb and into the room
Outa the water and into the air
I'm just a poorman's sunshine
from outa the water and into the air

Outa the shorts and into the long
Outa the shorts and into the long
Outa the grey and into the green
Outa the shorts and into the long
I'm just a poorman's sunshine
from outa the intro and into the song

Outa the school and into the wool
Outa the school and into the wool
Outa the in and into the out
Outa the school and into the wool
I'm just a poorman's sunshine
from outa the dumb into the shout

Outa the street and onto the stage
Outa the street and onto the stage
Outa ma head and onto the page
I'm just a poorman's sunshine
Outa the street and onto the stage

Outa the Lincoln and into the Lear
Outa the Lincoln and into the Lear
Out with the chicken and out with the beer
Outa the Lincoln and into the Lear
I'm just a poorman's sunshine
Outa the water and into the air

PROSE

Smuggler's Sunday

The sweet fragrance of serenity is broken only by the funny Plip! Plop! of water-drops hanging pregnant from the brass tap.

Such is the silence in the early morning kitchen.
The still life of objects lies sad in the grey misty light. Bead curtains sleep. Through them is the "Room." In there a sun-light shaft falls (a harpsichord sound) on to a carpet of Turkish Forestry, musky and dark.

Old lace work, dust and fur, moquette rugs and silk, velvet cushions, and old photographs and posters of vaudeville stars and Sarah Bernhardt are there.

A long ago funeral of lost faces in brown coats looks around for remembrance unheeded.

A huge stuffed bear stands halted in its dance, its marble eyes dull in the shadows. Powdered sun dust filters through the lace curtains, silence to silence in the golden reflection of the brass ball on the giant chariot bed. Silken tassels hang softly to the floor. An old Mariner's trunk sits under the bed, an old travelling ticket from Greece slowly fading out of sight. Great barbarian furs drape the resting place of the two sleepers. They lie as two children, their mouths open and warm, their arms lying in puppet gestures across one another. The velvet canopy casts a shadow on drowsy skin. Luici lies with a crown of black curls atop his peaceful features, a pencil moustache under his nose. Saffron lies curled in the fur womb with her thumb gently in her mouth, so . . .

The faint far away sound of running children filters into the room. A small pussy cat lies curled under Saffron's face, rising and falling softly in its "never-never land" sleep.

Saffron is a girl-child with funny straw hair and large eyes. Cut glass jewels adorn her slender fingers; her other hand holds a ruff of black Ostrich feathers around Luici's neck.

A Victorian telephone jangles into life in the still boudoir, the exchange is Notting Hill Gate. A Prince's hand reaches and takes the receiver into the soft feathers by his ear. In his drowsy confusion Luici speaks.

"Wadayawan?"

"What you want is easier" the voice said.

"Is's room service?"

"It's Sunday again" the voice laughed. Ha! Ha!

"Is air petrol in a motor?"

"Uhu!" the voice returned.

"Thirty minutes" said Luici, and the phone clicked with a deep pur-r-r.

The pussy cat opened its eyes, purred and went back to its dream. Luici poised the receiver over the tiny brass cradle and smashed it down.

The gulls were screaming above the roar of the sea as the black slinky Lagonda shifted on the windy coastal road. At the wheel was a strong looking man with sad beautiful eyes and a heavy moustache. He wore a rolled-necked sweater and a black double-breasted suit, blue ski-shades and white spats. The butt of his cigar rolled between his teeth. In the back sat Luici dressed in a light brown double-breasted suit with a candy striped shirt, gloves, cane, brimmed Bogart hat and brown and white Fred Astaire brogues. (See Vouge)

Saffron fidgets with heavily made-up eyes, in a bead dress, her legs folded under her like some beautiful imperial Afghan hound. She sticks her finger in a bag of sherbet and sucks it clean over and over again. The salty air rushes through her blonde helmet of hair.

The cigar hit the road, and the Lagonda swung off on to a grassy sand-dune and settled in. The sound of the sea remained. The surf-top stallions rode the green seas, disappearing in the far away horizon mist. The three disembarked, and the driver took a small brown suitcase and a rug from the boot, then over-took the other two on to the beach. He opened an imaginary door to the sand and bade Luici and Saffron to enter. She giggled and dabbed sherbet on her whetted finger and stuck it in Luici's mouth, which made him cough a little.

The driver was called Gypsy. A French-Moroccan who came to London town and lost his way to find Luici and Saffron. They met in a vast graveyard one winter's day, too long ago for words.

He spread the rug down and placed the small case on the sand. It had the initials G.A.S., embossed in gold on the top. Luici stabbed his cane in the sand, took off his hat, placed his gloves inside and put his hat on the silver carved cane top. Taking a pair of high-powered binoculars from Gypsy's big hand, he lay on his back and raised the glasses to his eyes. Two tiny shoes fell in the sand from Saffron's feet as she ran to the water's edge. The gulls dived nearer to his eyes on the two circular movie screens. Slowly he dropped the lenses to the ocean and to the sand. He laughed gently at Saffron splashing in the foam, lifting her skirts to the wind. He turned the glasses along the distant beach. A tiny speck became a moving thing and he held it in focus whilst the sound of glass and wine being poured came from behind. The speck became a tiny figure holding a small suitcase in his left hand and padding along the hard, damp sand. A blur came across the lenses and Luici lowered them to take the dark maroon liquid to his lips. He sipped.

He found the tiny figure again and distinguished his blowing yellow hair dancing in the sea-breezes. The figure wore a French trench coat, buttoned up tight, faded blue jeans and white sneaker boots with red laces. The figure grew and grew in the binoculars until the trench coat blacked out the light.

Luici put the glasses down in the sand and looked up at the gaunt young man standing beside him. The newcomer crouched down with his little case of gold initialled leather between his legs and smiled. "Hey" he said suddenly. "Feel good?" Luici smiled and nodded his head slowly. Gypsy filled the two used wine glasses and poured a third. All three took the nectar and drank. The blond boy tipped his above his open mouth, the tiny last dregs sprayed his teeth, he gargled once and swallowed.

The blond beachcomber was an old friend of Luici. He lived in a tiny wooden beach house along the shore beside the little pine forest on shark point. The roof was painted in tangerine pastel and a swordfish skeleton was nailed over the salt worn door.

A gull screamed and was stifled by the wind flapping the trench coat with sharp cracks. Luici dug his wine glass in the sand and made a sand pie; Altar to the Sky, and the sand bird's eye. Jonathan opened his tiny case to reveal a package wrapped in tough brown paper, tied with white string and sealed with red wax. He took it out and handed it to Gypsy who placed it in his small case. At the same time Luici withdrew a large bundle of money from his coat and gave it to Jonathan who let it float into his case, quickly trapping the coloured paper. Jonathan rose to his feet; the other two did likewise. The faint sound of giggling turned the three heads to the waving sand-dunes. Saffron came over the rise, her arms great with flowers and sea-shells. She joined the rest. "Hello Jonathan" she smiled. "How is Melanie?"

"Just fine and pregnant" Jonathan answered.

"Give her my love" Saffron said as she took a beach flower and put it in Jonathan's button-hole. She stepped back to form a line with Gyp and Luici.

The sea sounded again and again, wrath of moon.

Jonathan waved slightly and turned with his tiny case, polishing itself against his leg. He hesitated and said, "nice wine."

Gypsy picked up the wine bottle, juggled it once and threw it to Jonathan who caught and juggled it also. He turned as he caught it and started his clumsy sand-walk to his meal of steamed mackerel in the tiny beach hut.

The Lagonda wound along the coast highway into Mousehole-by-the-Sea. The shiny wet promenade lay deserted with winter time weather. Wind-blown stragglers fought in the mini-gale, far too busy to notice the old-fashioned saloon car hissing on the rained-on road. The driver halted the motor car at a steamed-up cafe, with TEAS in giant letters on the corrugated roof.

Saffron ran up the concrete steps to the door, her head buried in a bushy fur coat. Luici shook the glass door open, allowing the winds of the sea to burst in and investigate the farthest corners. The dead-pan Tea Lady looked at the intruders with an extremely tired stare. Gulls echoed above the little shack. The glass door crashed shut, shutting out the pounding of the breakers. The only other occupant was a fresh looking old man steaming his beard over tan-coloured tea. A big silver tea machine hissed and spluttered. The bleached-out Tea Lady poured three large white cups of steam in silence and spilled the last one on the coins Luici had thrown on the counter. Saffron stuck her elbow in Luici's ribs, holding back a burst of her beautiful laughter. All three held their amusement down to a twitching smile and seated themselves at the misty window.

They drank the tea, the wind nearly smashing the glass door as they left.

The next day back in London, Saffron walked the crowded market street, buying food and sweets to fill their stomachs for strength to play. The brightly coloured fruit stores shone into her wide eyes. She picked up the soft tissue paper that fruits are wrapped in and put some in her straw bag to show to Luici. She bought all kinds of goodies and made it back to Oliver Road. Three children played in the road as she turned the corner. Recognising the youngest, Saffron shouted "hello" to which the child smiled and shouted back in slurred infant words, indistinguishable from jazz.

No. 15 stood in front of her. She stretched with her little brass key and opened the heavy stained glass door to the mosaic hallway. The light was faint, the air a little chilled. The brass fittings sparkled in the gloom. Tiny stars glinted in the granite steps as she scuffed and made giant leaps up to the floor where the lift began. She closed the black wrought-iron lift gates and rode the box of mirrors to the Fourth Floor. The cosy little room offered its comfort to her, and as she entered she sighed with visible relief. She clonked her groceries on the sink top in the tiny kitchen and looked through the chattering bead curtains to her man. Luici sat in a big rocking chair quietly talking to the cat lying in his lap. Saffron smiled ever so slightly with her big grey eyes.

"Hey Baby" Luici said.
"Hey" Saffron whispered and she made a love gesture with her fingers. Leaning down she kissed his head.
"It's best you put on a collar and go."

"Incident"

I went down to the sea. It was roaring and crashing and thoroughly foul. I turned my back in disgust and decided to return home.

I arrived at the seaside station in plenty of time and bought my ticket across the polished oak.

I needed a porter. I'd purchased a few old books.

At the gate I asked the inspector for a porter. He called up on the phone and the young long haired junior porter answered "Yes, what is it?"
"Wadayamean wat is it! Work! you've got a job to do," shouted the inspector.

After a young nylon overalled waitress had asked and been given an autograph on a paper napkin, a large fat clown of a woman came over. She had dyed cotton blonde hair. Her face was scarred with a glossy crimson mouth which said.

"Who's Donoban, are you Donoban?"
"I am Donovan," I said.
"You're in the music business aintcha?"
"Yes"
Then she nonchalantly asked.
"Do you know Liberace?"
"No"
"I was with him in the old days, I was his first sweetheart."
I turned to escape from her clown smiling pulp of a face.

"Are you fit?" I nodded at the junior porter, who stood, a hood if ever there was. His station hat was pushed back over his long hair.

A faded blue denim station jacket hung loose on his thin frame. Bell bottomed faded jeans and high heeled points completed him.
Spotty, he said, "Yeah."

The face spoke again, "Well goodbye Donoban."

She held out her little fat white fingers. It was an old drunk's trick, and I fell for it.

I put down my parcel and took her hand.

"If you ever (pause) see Lib (pause) tell him (pause) Olive still loves him and thinks of him always." She accentuated certain words by pulling down on my held hand.

I tried withdrawing but her grip tightened.

"Now you tell him that," she added, "when you see him." "Okay," said I, "but I don't think I'll ever." But she didn't hear, because she faded away from my vision to the right, fox trotting with a small time band leader in blazer and bags, at the mirror ballroom in a pre-war photograph.

I picked up my books and passed through the gate, the inspector squeezed my arm. The junior porter took to the stairs, he told me of some American girls who were mad about me. I got on the train, gave him half a crown and sat down to write this.

Cardiff — Swansea '67

Prayer of Thanks

I thank the Queen of Living Things
for showing me each day
All the pretty beauty things
living in her day

And I thank her kindly for
bestowing upon me
The simple gift to daily lift
my tiny eyes to see